Country Weekend Homes

Country Weekend Homes

Author
Cristina Montes

Editor
Paco Asensio

Photos

© Phillippe Saharoff: **The feel of yesteryear**

© G. de Chabaneix (ACI Roca-Sastre): **Seduced by the past,**
   Mediterranean refuge

© Ricardo Labougle: **A farmhouse amid the sunflowers, Classical inspiration,**
   The perfect hideaway, A magical cabin, A play of contrasts,
   Order and harmony

© Pere Peris: **Minimum expression**

© Pere Planells: **Captivating tranquility, The spirit of the millennium, The little**
   Alhambra, An artists' retreat, Hidden in a garden, The power
   of serenity, Pure style, A renewal of tradition, Peerless simplicity

Translation
Harry Paul

Editing and proof reading
Wendy Griswold and Julie King

Art director
Mireia Casanovas Soley

Graphic design and layout
Emma Termes Parera

2001 © Loft Publications S.L. and HBI,
an imprint of HarperCollins Publishers

First published in 2001 by LOFT and HBI,
an imprint of HarperCollins Publishers
10 East 53rd St. New York, NY 10022-5299

Distributed in the U.S. and Canada by Watson-Guptill Publications
770 Broadway New York, NY 10003-9595
Telephone: (800) 451-1741 or (732) 363-4511 in NJ, AK, HI Fax: (732) 363-0338

Distributed throughout the rest of the world by
HarperCollins International
10 East 53rd St. New York, NY 10022-5299
Fax: (212) 207-7654

Hardcovert ISBN: 0-06-620933-1
Paperback ISBN: 0-8230-0969-6
D.L.: B-21.847-2001

Printed in Spain

If you want to make any suggestions for work to be included in our forthcoming books, please e-mail us at
loft@loftpublications.com

Introduction

Everyone has a picture in their mind of green fields extending as far as the eye can see, peaceful meadows, fresh air and clear, never-ending blue skies.These are idyllic scenes for stressed-out city dwellers who must battle every day with noise, pollution, and traffic jams.

Anyone who has to put up with the din and chaos of a city wants a place in the country where he can forget it all. That's why more and more people are making their dream of country life come true by buying, building, or restoring a second residence far from the asphalt jungle.

This book includes weekend retreats in six countries: Argentina, Uruguay, Morocco, France, the United States and Spain. In addition to illustrating different architectural approaches and lifestyles, it offers a range of practical solutions and ideas for anyone who is thinking about buying or remodeling a second home.

After seeing these projects, one thing is obvious: it's not where you start that matters. Seemingly unpromising structures can be turned into wonderful homes. This book features everything from a 375-square-foot cabin in the woods and a spacious turn of the century riyadh in old Marrakesh, to a farmhouse made of recycled materials and typical Mediterranean country homes, among others. There are endless possibilities for the structure, the exterior finishing, and the interior decoration. It's basically up to the person who lives there. But the key design goals should be comfort and warmth. The house should be a refuge; the superfluous luxuries we find it so hard to live without in our primary residences should be left behind. This is an important step toward regaining inner harmony.

Another characteristic these homes have in common is their disregard for the whims of fashion. They generally appear to be timeless, exquisitely simple, and immensely practical. Although there are obvious differences, their common objective is to provide a peaceful, quiet place for those precious days of leisure. In these havens, we seek to enrich ourselves, delight in the beautiful setting, return to nature, and get in step with the rhythm of the seasons. In these places, that rhythm is clear. It's found in the land, the colors, the fragrances, the textures... a celebration of the senses. We need to make the most of these revitalizing moments, when we slow down to nature's speed.

Without a doubt, all of these homes give their owners the opportunity to live life at a slower pace, to be happier, more human, and more intimately in touch with nature, even if it's just on weekends.

Cristina Montes

A farmhouse amid the sunflowers

Curios, antiques, collectors' items, and old furniture come together in this charming country home, where there's room for everything.

Williamsport, Pennsylvania, USA

Initially intended as a temporary refuge for the owner this project, Aaron Hojman, while his permanent home was being constructed, ended up as a country house which boasts all of today's modern conveniences while retaining the charm of bygone years.

This 861–square–foot farmhouse is located in the countryside near Williamsport, Pennsylvania. In this nearly isolated setting, one is reminded of the existence of the outside world only when a vehicle passes on the narrow road nearby.

The house, inspired by the railway station storehouses designed at the end of the nineteenth century by the English and clearly reminiscent of granaries in California and the Northeastern U.S., was constructed out of rusted metal sheeting bought at auctions of no-longer-needed train stations.

The house, hidden by sunflowers in a landscape of soft, rolling green hills, has an ephemeral feeling that harks back to its origins.

The way the house was built and the decor make it seem as if the dwelling has been there for ages, although it is really just three years old. Inside, the rooms, full but not cluttered, are like improvised museums, with all sorts of objects, some unusual, like the doors of the art cinema which the owner frequented in his youth, or a bust of Garibaldi from a Montevideo café.

The windows, also acquired at auction, break the harshness of the facade and permit natural light to bathe the rooms, which are meticulously and eclectically decorated to evoke the past.

The labor of love that went into the search for the furniture and other items that are full of history and memories, and the style with which they are arranged, have created a delightful, charming home.

Tucked away inside this farmhouse, which at first sight appears to be in ruins, are lovingly cared-for rooms filled with memories, rooms which make you feel at home.

The green wooden chairs are an old type widely used in South American hotels. The wooden floor of the house's entryway is made of old planks from the platform behind a bar in a café.

A jumble of things. This is a fair description of this delightful house, where one finds everything from a set of china used many years ago in an elegant hotel to a German globe with a fascinating but sad history. A family of Jews forced to flee Berlin in the Thirties gave it to the owner more than 30 years ago.

This diagonal entryway, with its numerous panes of glass, was purchased at an auction. The owner's enthusiasm for salvaging and restoring intriguing objects is also reflected in the exterior of the house.

Scattered about the house are countless objects steeped in the past, like this collection of wooden stoppers for wine barrels, displayed on the heavy dining room table.

A room had to be set up next to the house where the owner could store secondhand items he picked up as he traveled around the country in his van.

Classical inspiration

A forceful elegance reminiscent of the past is the appeal of this home, which tries to hide amid the immensity of nature.

Santa Rosa, Argentina

The architect for this project, Jacques Bedel, used admirable restraint in designing this house surrounded by the vast openness of the Argentinean Pampas.

The walls and columns, which form a central plaza that emphasizes the lines of the modest-looking building, are the only visible features establishing the boundary between the living space and the land.

The grasslands stretching out into the distance and the austere, rectangularity of the house make it the center of attention and enhance its unadorned beauty. The meticulous structural symmetry produces clearly defined interiors. In the center is a large living room, which is surrounded at each corner by the other four rooms: the kitchen, a study, and two bedrooms with baths.

The house is constructed of pre-fabricated polyethylene sheets, a novel material with great insulating capacity, which is also used for the roof, together with concrete beams. The flooring is a concrete slab. The cornice, which continues all around the building, gives the terraces a gallery–like appearance.

Inside the house, two fireplaces divide the spacious living/dining room. A pile of logs reinforces the separation. The dignified atmosphere is enhanced by the combination of classical-style furniture and contemporary pieces. The result is a cozy home full of elegance and character.

> The solid geometric lines of this building, brightened by the colors employed and the large windows along the entire facade, provide a pleasing contrast to the surrounding countryside.

To give the rooms a personal feel, the designer updated a classical style with contemporary elements. The solemn, dark tone of much of the furniture is broken by the colorful decorative accents.

The swimming pool is surrounded by a brick walk. The color harmony, the built-in underwater stairs, and the discreet trim create visual continuity.

Bougainvillea grow in large clay pots next to the sheltering brick walls, creating a rich display of color.

The bathroom furnishings are simple and functional and lacquered in white, which makes the room seem larger and brighter.

The perfect hideaway

This residence shows what can be achieved when you attain a balance of modern elements, nature, and tradition. Relaxed design and a peaceful setting create the perfect spot for getting away from it all

Avignon, France

Surrounded by wilderness, buried deep in a thick forest in France, this home is the ideal place for leaving one's cares behind in the city and enjoying nature.

Built on a concrete base, this two–story house designed by architect Martín G. Pustilnick is made of treated pine insulated with polyurethane panels so it can be enjoyed year–round.

On two sides, a wooden porch welcomes visitors to while away the long summer evenings. An attractive mix of country tradition and modern style characterizes the ground floor living room and kitchen. The bedroom and bath on the second floor complete the 732-square-foot living space, certainly not large, but well-proportioned and fully utilized.

> The facade is an expressive contrast of red and green, a combination often found in nature.

As you come through the front door, the kitchen is on your left and on the right is the type of living room where you just want to settle in and enjoy the outside views. These rooms are visually separated by the staircase opposite the entryway, which leads up to the second floor and is integrated into the living room by shelves attached to the partition.

All the furniture in the house is simple and functional. Because space is at a premium, there are no unnecessary elements. Everything has a purpose. The features contributing to the house's comfortable ambience were designed on site; local craftsmen developed and executed many of the ideas. The homey simplicity is mirrored in the colors used: natural tones and a conservative palette with just a few striking touches.

A wooden deck leads to the main entrance. To the left you can see the kitchen shelving, which provides sufficient storage space.

Residents can relax and enjoy the fresh air on the porch at the rear of the house. As in the rest of the house, wood, properly treated to protect it against the weather, was used here for both the flooring and the furniture.

The furnishings in the bathroom, like everywhere else in the house, were designed to minimize clutter. Everything was made to measure so it would fit snugly. Below a window, the wash basin was built into a curved counter, with shelving for towels underneath.

A magical cabin

This small but cozy cottage that looks like something out of a fairy tale is full of surprises.

Punta del Este, Uruguay

This crisp-lined cabin designed by Juan Ricci is located in a forest clearing near Punta del Este, Uruguay, where the beauty of the wilderness is combined with a carefully manicured garden. A partially-covered porch, used as an outdoor living area, leads to the main room, where white wooden surfaces predominate. Introducing large pieces of furniture into this neutral background not only makes the room seem bigger but also provides a tranquil, rustic air.

Two white, old-fashioned, iron single beds stand harmoniously opposite a wider, dark wooden bed which serves as a sofa during the day. The versatile living area is marked off by a coffee table and two wicker chairs on a bright orange rug. In one corner, behind a screen, is a dressing area and a large but unobtrusive wooden armoire. Next to it, on a purple rug, is a simple wooden chair, also painted white, to sit on when putting on riding boots. The immaculately white dining area is opposite. Here, the only touch of color is provided by the blue stripes in the curtains, a pattern repeated on the bedspreads, while the screen has a blue plaid pattern.

The living area contains only essential furniture. The fabrics, rugs, and a few decorative elements provide the color which gives life to the neutral background.

Even in such a simple country cabin, much can be achieved with the judicious use of unpretentious decorative features. The key to the color balance lies in the eclectic collection of furniture, rugs, and fabrics contrasted against the neutral background. As a result, this micro-space is a great spot for spending family weekends enjoying nature without forgoing the pleasures of modern life.

This cabin in the middle of a forest shows how comfortable life can be with only the bare essentials. In the functional interior, every element has its own special place. The decor and lack of partitions, with everything in one room, makes the most of the available space.

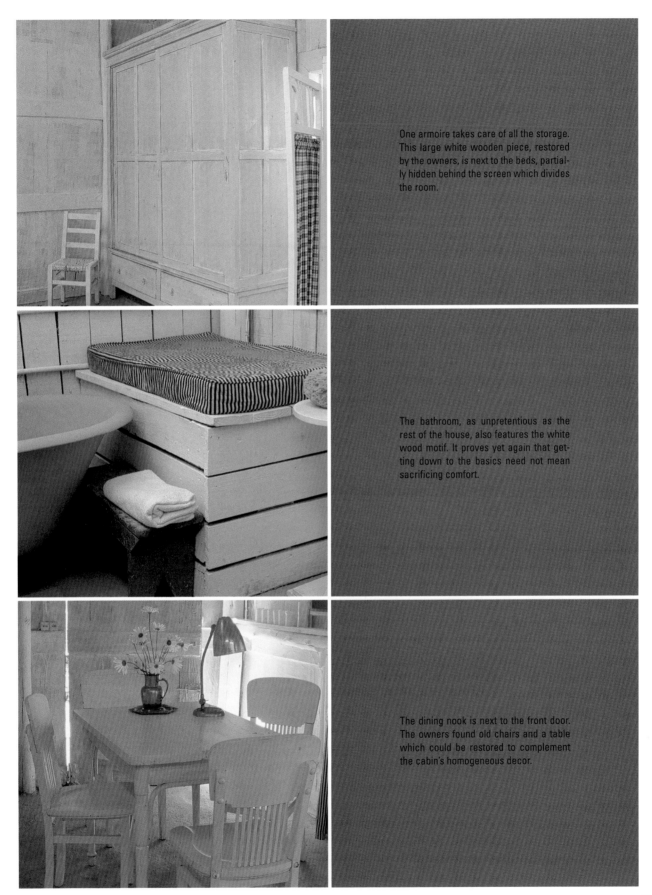

One armoire takes care of all the storage. This large white wooden piece, restored by the owners, is next to the beds, partially hidden behind the screen which divides the room.

The bathroom, as unpretentious as the rest of the house, also features the white wood motif. It proves yet again that getting down to the basics need not mean sacrificing comfort.

The dining nook is next to the front door. The owners found old chairs and a table which could be restored to complement the cabin's homogeneous decor.

A play of contrasts

The subtle, meticulous design of this spacious home hidden away in the countryside slowly wins you over

Firenze, Italy

This Italian house is an intelligent synthesis of the traditional and the modern.

Actually two buildings connected by a patio and a long, covered porch next to the swimming pool, this home had to be large to avoid getting lost amid the immensity of its natural setting. The main building, which opens onto the porch, contains the common areas: the living room, kitchen, and dining room. The bedrooms, guest quarters, and bathrooms are located in the annex.

The facade is painted a deep salmon color, providing a contrast with the green vegetation, the blue of the pool, and the gray uralite roof. The combination of textures and colors forms an attractive chromatic play of contrasts. The walls of both buildings are filled with windows, framed in green varnished wood, which allow the inhabitants to feast their eyes on nature while the sunlight floods every corner.

A spectacular landscape and lush vegetation are the setting for this exquisitely simple home with a harmonious blend of colors and textures.

The interior has plenty of open space for balance and a smooth, natural flow of energy. The deliberately underfurnished rooms bring the beauty of the architecture to the fore and can only be described as refined spaces with an unusual mix of textures and styles from different periods.

All in all, it is a relaxing home in both structure and appearance. Here one can luxuriate in the stillness of the countryside while enjoying all the modern comforts a place in the city can offer.

The unbroken row of appliances accentuates the roominess of the kitchen. Low, white, wooden, glass-paneled cupboards run along the windows, beneath a long marble work counter. In the middle of the room, an old wooden table adds a rustic touch to a kitchen with an otherwise industrial feel.

In one of the living rooms a cozy area has been set up in front of the fireplace, which is built into a section of the wall decorated in a contrasting color. High above, a window frames the landscape outside and allows more natural light to enter.

Enormous windows and eclectic color, texture, and style combinations are found throughout. The ochre walls and the green door and window frames intensify the already extraordinary luminosity.

Carefully selected details add personal touches. In one of the dining rooms, this unique, restored glass lamp hangs from three iron chains. Its beauty is enhanced by the contrast with the wooden rafters.

Order and harmony

There is no place for curves in this home. Order, simplicity, and straight lines are its defining characteristics.

Punta del Este, Uruguay

The geometric lines of this building in Punta del Este, Uruguay, contrast with the wild, uneven surrounding landscape. If nature seems out of control, the feeling passes, thanks to the cream color used inside and out.

The exterior of the residence is utterly austere. A simple wooden deck and a flowerpot grace the entrance. No other architectural features interfere with the simplicity. This apparent coldness is balanced by warm wood and rattan furniture on the terrace at the rear of the house.

This large building has an external structure reminiscent of a Rubik's cube. Everything is smooth and flat. The uniformly recessed, rectangular windows and the plain, monochrome walls reinforce the homogeneity.

However, what is restrained and unassuming on the outside becomes colorful and contrasting on the inside. The outer door leads into a living room neatly divided in two. The decor is symmetrical. Sofas, lamps, chairs, and other pieces are repeated on both sides. It is as if one were looking at a reflection in a mirror. Yet the contrasts are the most striking elements. The dark blue of the sofas sets off the intense red of the carpet and the green of the curtains. The result is eye-catching and suggestive. Classic pieces of furniture share the space with modern designs, creating aesthetically pleasing rooms and providing visual relief from the strict order that is the hallmark of the house.

The functionality, the vitality and power of the colors, and the contrasts work together to create a home with a style all its own.

> At the rear of the house, a terrace functions as an open-air living room. The warm furniture contrasts with the restrained facade.

The dignified geometry and order are broken by the color contrasts and other details, producing serene, fresh, and, above all, functional rooms.

A neutral cream tone is the dominant color throughout the house, ensuring decorative continuity. This set of glass balls in different sizes and colors, placed on a ledge by the staircase, is an original touch.

The steps in the staircase leading up to the second floor bedrooms, are so long that one hardly notices the climb. They are also in perfect harmony with the rest of the house.

The vibrant colors are striking and highly alluring against the cream-colored bedroom wall. Here, as everywhere else, there is plenty of light and nothing superfluous. Only the essential is included.

Captivating tranquility

This Moorish house is like an oasis at the end of a long journey: the perfect place to forget fast-paced Western living and to enjoy the good things of life.

Marrakech, Morocco

Architect Charles Bocarra designed this house that has a modern spirit but was inspired by typical Moroccan structures.

On the outskirts of Marrakech, surrounded by palm trees and golf courses, it evokes the past with fresh, sharp lines that are far removed from the limitations of Western architecture.

The living room, dining room, several bedrooms, and a terrace with a small swimming pool occupy the first of the three floors. The second floor contains large balconies and the master bedroom, with its own parlor, complete with fireplace, and the master bath. The top floor is a roomy area, open to the elements, with numerous Arabic decorative motifs.

Inside are grand high-ceilinged rooms, some vaulted and others coffered. Ceramic-tiled, patterned floors with borders, sometimes covered with kilims, provide a rich mix of styles that are accented by the strong natural lighting.

The walls are painted in various colors, according to the room and its function. The living rooms, entrance hall, dining room, and other common areas, as well as the master bedroom, are a majestic salmon. In another bedroom, a cold bluish gray contrasts with the alluring wood of the ceiling.

This ochre-walled terrace is ready for quiet relaxation in woven-reed chairs. Once you get settled, you won't want to be disturbed.

The bathrooms are a vibrant ochre, which is picked up in the floor and wall tiles. In a house like this, the abundant natural light highlights the colors inside. The result here is a distinctive consistency which nonetheless allows the differences to shine through.

The interior decoration, discreet, refined, and exquisite, is built around Eastern-style furniture and accent pieces as well as more European, modern pieces crafted by local artisans. The successful mix of styles and trends serves as a reminder that predictability can be disavowed.

The red setting sun casts wonderful shadows that make you forget everyday hassles and the daily routine.

An ancient wooden door studded with iron and brass welcomes you inside, where you are bathed in rich colors, fragrances, and textures.

The nightstand in this bedroom is a hand-crafted Moorish piece that was restored to its original splendor. The dark tones and the heavy wood contrast with the delicate candle holder and the pale shade of the walls.

The ceilings in some rooms have typical Moorish coffering. The restored lamp, in all its beauty, was discovered by the owners in an antique shop.

An unassuming, stylishly-colored border runs around this small swimming pool. The same pattern, repeated on the bottom, can be seen through the crystal-clear water.

The spirit of the millennium

Exuding the charm of a welcoming, fascinating city,
this house is steeped in more than 100 years of history.

Marrakech, Morocco

This late 19th century riyadh is tucked away in the heart of Marrakech, but its treasures are there for anyone who enters its doors. The rooms surround a central courtyard, which is typical of this part of the world. Those responsible for the renovation were as faithful as possible to the original design and respected the house's special features. The only addition was a contemporary bedroom suite.

Captivated by the Moorish style and aware that this culture venerates water as the source of life, the owners decided to install a small swimming pool, part of which is covered, and to preserve the traditional Moroccan hammam.

The renovation retained the original three levels. The ground floor houses living rooms, salons, the dining room, and the kitchen. A room decorated with mementos from foreign trips, the new bedroom, and several baths are on the second floor. The top level features a large terrace with spectacular views of the seductive city calmly going about its daily routine or sparkling under the cloudless night sky.

> All the rooms open onto the central courtyard and are understated because the architecture requires no enhancement.

Light reaches every part of the house, moving through diaphanous interiors that take a back seat to the stately, timeless architecture unmatched by modern forms and lines. The rooms, which flow together while remaining separate, contain many pieces obtained from a local dealer in antiques. Styles are subtly combined to create a distinctive, suggestive atmosphere and make this home a delightful leisure retreat.

An intelligently-planned mixture of past and present gives this home character and ensures that, although the years may pass, its charm will remain intact.

The coffered ceiling, the ceramic tiles on many walls, the arches, and the solid wood doors with their inscriptions are some of the features which bear witness to the age of the house and its ancient memories.

On the ground floor, the exquisitely austere hammam. The room is distinguished by the stone washstand, a niche in one of the walls, and a high, painted ceiling.

Despite some updating in the kitchen, its 19th century flavor remains. The design is unpretentious, functional, and tranquil.

The owners of the house, who are in love with sub-Saharan Africa, visit there as often as they can. One of the rooms is decorated with mementos from their trips. However, the African theme is not repeated in the bedroom suite, which is decorated in a contemporary European style.

Aware that the ceilings in all of the rooms are genuine works of art, the owners made sure that they would be carefully preserved so the splendid craftsmanship and painting could be appreciated.

Another engaging architectural feature is the facade, with its restored antique doors and windows. These decorative elements remind us of the splendor of the past and befit a house so full of character.

In the kitchen, a small handcrafted cabinet displays a fabulous collection of Moroccan ceramics from each region of the country. These little ornaments embellish and add a touch of color to an otherwise austere, simple room.

The little Alhambra

A marvel with countless architectural secrets, this house boldly proclaims its sources of inspiration, defying the passage of time.

El palmeral, Marrakech, Morocco

Charles Boccara, an architect seduced by the sensuality and refinement of Morocco, designed this vacation home in a Moorish style, using traditional local construction methods.

The roomy house, in the Palm Gardens on the outskirts of Marrakech, is a fine example of how structures from the past can be reinvented and adapted without losing either their charm or significance.

Light, air, and water are all important architectural factors and, indeed, the design often focuses on these elements to heighten the overall sensation of tranquility and to exploit the potential of the natural setting.

Light, undeniably a key ingredient, transforms every room, making the walls shimmer. In the baths and in the salon, complete with fireplace, light filters through openings in the vaulted ceiling. This converts the walls and ceiling into a dynamic geometric composition which invites you to marvel at the way the luminescence accentuates some shapes and minimizes others.

A row of columns beckons visitors from the garden to the house and supports a balcony. It is one of many points of easy access to the ground floor.

The serene, open interior rooms are a compromise between the elegance that is only fitting in a home like this and the owners' desire to employ their own good taste and discretion. The contemporary furniture, pictures, and accessories are, for the most part, imported from France. They blend comfortably with pieces designed by Bocarra himself and manufactured in Morocco using traditional methods.

Handicrafts and restored antiques provide a final touch. The message of this sensually gratifying house is that order and unity are not everything.

In many areas of the garden, water flows continuously. This pool at the rear of the property, surrounded by thick vegetation, is characteristically Moorish.

A small garden annex with guest bedrooms echoes the style of the main building.

A grand arch separates one of the living rooms from the dining room, which features giant floor-to-ceiling windows and glass doors leading to the garden and pond.

The neutral quality of the salmon-colored background is broken by this curvy chaise-longue. Above, in a space between rooms, stands a European sculpture of a ballerina.

Light enters from above in some rooms. Here, a magnificent adobe structure is topped by a glass dome, creating a fascinating play of light and shadow.

Water is found in many corners of the property. Ceramic tiles in a geometric pattern border this stone fountain in the garden.

The various outside doors are highly valuable, antique originals restored by the owner to add a personal touch to the walls.

Seduced by the past

This house in the middle of a lush garden, surrounded by mountains, is a superb combination of past and present.

Corsica, Italy

All the comforts of this house, which overlooks a village on the French island of Corsica, are twenty-fist century. But, standing firm against the passage of time, the dwelling was renovated using traditional methods.

The architect responsible for the project, Colombe Stevens, traveled around the island to immerse himself in local construction techniques and applied them to this subtly modernized house. The result is impeccable.

The floors were reorganized and the rooms redistributed. Knowing that the feeling of bygone days has a charm all its own, Stevens adhered to classic approaches instead of using acrylic paints and other expedients. In the process, the architect created an attractive house with a brilliant variety of styles, materials, and textures.

A tall Cyprus tree next to the steps is prominent in the garden filled with olive trees, yews, and various bushes and shrubs. The lush green contrasts with the stone walls, ochre facade, white window and door frames, and gray shutters.

Approaching the house from the garden, after climbing the stone staircase, you come to a facade with neat, shuttered windows through which you can glimpse bright rooms where white and ochre tones predominate, just as on the outside. The whole interior is constantly bathed in strong Mediterranean sunlight.

The other side of the house contains two terraces from which you can gaze down on the beautiful church and narrow streets while you enjoy a relaxing supper, chat, or just rest. A reed covering provides relief from the summer heat and walls on three sides afford shelter from the cool winter breezes.

Inside, the furniture is distinctly colonial, but there are also rustic, Eastern, and contemporary pieces. It is a seductive mix with a personal touch, dazzling and timeless, befitting this jewel of an island.

The desire for simplicity and the rejection of luxuries guided the choice of room decor. The blending of styles, materials, colors, and textures reveals a deep respect for local tradition. The result is a house with personality and an appreciation for the past.

During the day, this lamp and outcropping of rock from the original structure cast captivating shadows on the wall. At night, the lamp lights up the terrace below.

In this bathroom, a niche above the sink provides a handy storage place for soap and other toiletries.

This large gray cement partition has a dual role: a headboard for the bed and a divider which hides the small shower and wash basin behind it.

Mediterranean refuge

Enchanting and full of personality, this modest home is an ideal place for getting in touch with nature.

Lubèron, France

Lovingly restored by its owners, this house south of Lubéron in France manages to fit all the necessary comforts into its 410 square feet.

The renovation converted what was originally an outbuilding for the storage of farm equipment into the perfect spot for spending those long, hot summer vacations when the blue skies beckon, or just weekends forgetting the daily grind.

Perched on a pedestal-like cement base surrounded by a typically Mediterranean landscape, this little home preserves the flavor of local tradition in every sense. The architect retained the existing structure and made every effort to get the details right. The window frames and doors were painted a bluish gray to set them off against the light tones of the stone walls and cement floor. A small reservoir behind the building, previously used for watering crops, was turned into a swimming pool. Next to the entrance, on top of the base, a little terrace serves as an outdoor living room.

The doors and abundant windows let in plenty of light and fresh air; the modest dimensions are not a problem.

There are no partitions inside: everything is integrated into one room. Furniture establishes the confines of the various functional areas. All the walls, except those adjoining the ochre-colored dining area, were painted white to enhance the light and make the space seem larger.

The room is sparsely but naturally furnished with rustic antique and secondhand pieces that are put to full use. A warm house is not necessarily a cluttered house.

Authentic country kitchens are the inspiration for this room. There are no luxuries, not even electrical appliances, and the rural spirit is evident in the simplicity of the furniture and the materials used, down to the smallest detail.

The shower curtain hangs from a varnished branch, a novel touch which exemplifies the owners' desire to imbue the house with a natural atmosphere.

Cupboards would take up space, so wall niches, which are nearly unnoticeable because of the chromatic continuity, provide a practical solution.

This subtle, nearly invisible glass hanger helps keep the room neat and tidy. Ostentatious accessories would be out of place here.

The feel of yesteryear

The restoration and expansion of this weekend home preserved the enchantment of the original building while bringing it up-to-date.

L'ile de Ré, France

Originally, this house had only one room on the ground floor and a bedroom upstairs. But after ten years of painstaking renovation, it now has four bedrooms and plenty of space for friends, children, and even grandchildren. The key to the project was connecting an old toolshed to the main part of the home. Now, with everything painted white, the passageway between the two structures is hardly noticeable. The only traces of the old structure are the small windows, the low ceilings, and the wooden staircase, all contributing to the home's rural character.

Soft pastel tones personalize the interior of this residence, situated on France's Île de Ré. The minute you cross the threshold you notice the ceiling painted a very light gray, the same shade used on all the woodwork, including the porches and window frames. A contrasting pale forest green was selected for the rustic kitchen units. On the ground floor is a completely white room with direct access to the garden. In one corner, next to a large, white, visually-integrated cupboard is a small porcelain washstand reminiscent of long-ago rural customs and lifestyles.

A pleasant little open-air breakfast nook occupies a quiet corner. The dark furniture contrasts with the light wall in the background.

On the top floor, up the restored staircase, are the bedrooms. The master bedroom suite has three rooms: the sleeping quarters, a wood-paneled bathroom painted in two shades of white, and a small sparsely-furnished study in a grayish blue tone, conducive to reading and quiet reflection.

This house proudly displays its roots and rural character.
The simple lines, the discreet colors and materials, and the unpretentious
furnishings are charming and welcoming.

The rooms contain
functional country-style
furniture. Floral
patterns, wooden chairs
and tables, natural
fabrics, and simple
designs predominate.

Throughout the house are engaging little corners: wooden bookshelves near a window, a small table attached to the wall, and a rattan chair-everything needed to have a space suitable for reading or writing.

The well-placed furniture makes the most of the available space without clutter or congestion. Everything has its own place and tidying is easy.

This country house, with its whitewashed walls, stone floors, relaxing colors, and comfortable, restrained furniture, is full of life, a great spot for recharging one's batteries on weekends.

An artists' retreat

Far from the hustle and bustle of the city, this is the ideal spot to let your imagination run wild. The restless spirit of the artists who stay here is ever-present.

Saignon in Lubèron, France

Located in the heart of Saignon, a town north of Lubéron in France, this home belongs to two art lovers, Pierre Jaccaud and Kamila Regent. On weekends, they are only too glad to open it up to talented artists who share their passion and who need a tranquil place where they can create.

It is a large building, but the owners were not tempted to clutter up the generous space with excessive furniture. Works of art by the owners and their friends enhance the tasteful decor.

All of the rooms contain contemporary pieces and some of the ceiling and wall frescoes are by famous artists, such as the Belgian Koen Theys. The plastic arts are part of the owners' daily lives. This ties in nicely with another of their passions, cooking, which is evident after one glance at the carefully designed kitchen. They often invite family and friends to savor the truffles and other regional specialties that they prepare themselves.

A long wooden table and lightweight chairs have been placed in a corner of the garden: an ideal setting for fresh air, good conversation, and fine food.

The kitchen is on the ground floor together with the dining room, a large living room gallery, and two other rooms. Although there is central heating, some of the rooms have fireplaces to make them more cozy. The second floor has three bedrooms and a reading room, separated by a wide corridor that leads to two bathrooms. Many original features were preserved. The wooden door frames and window trimming looked good, so why change them? Old and new have been combined harmoniously, using a minimalist approach.

Ochre and similar tones were used for the walls of the bedrooms, which may be alike in color but not in style and character. No two bedrooms are the same, but all complement each other to unify the second story. Typical Provencal ceramic tile was used for the flooring, and the bathrooms, dec-

orated in blue, still have the original fixtures and design. The owners did the restoration work themselves and were not inclined to change anything as long as the rooms were comfortable and welcoming.

Luminous, open-plan studios, where the owners or their visitors can easily find inspiration, occupy the entire third floor. The house has a total of four studios, three inside and one outside, the latter being used mainly by artists working with heavy or noisy materials.

A beautiful, well-tended garden, accessed through a passageway, makes it easy for the artists to step out for some fresh air, and rounds off this well-appointed but carefree weekend retreat.

All of the rooms have different decors. This meants that each space has its own personal, unconventional atmosphere.

Each bedroom is stylistically unique. The one with ochre tones is extremely bright but almost Spartan: an iron bed and two armchairs have the space all to themselves. In another, the color choice is bolder: red, fuchsia, and acid green stand out against the neutral walls and the conservative furniture.

Detail of the table in the garden. The right ingredients add up to a soft, relaxed atmosphere.

An astute blend of styles ensures warm, attractive rooms. The red of the armchair, the orange of the walls, and the strength of the wood are unbeatable. The natural light filtered by the mesh curtains further enhances the luminosity of this eclectic room.

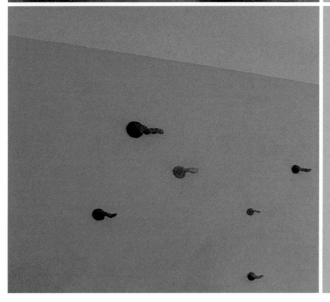

The owners decided to commission artists to decorate some of the rooms. One example of their work is this composition by Koen Theys, consisting of small, irregularly shaped splashes of color on the ochre-colored wall.

Minimum expression

Basic minimalist principles were skillfully applied to the renovation of this old restaurant, perfectly illustrating the saying that less is more

Pals, Girona, Spain

Renounce everything superfluous. Refine the space as much as possible to reach an emptiness: an emptiness that is full. These are the premises that guided interior designers Cristina Rodríguez and Augusto Le Monnier when they transformed this run-down restaurant in Girona, Spain into a charming home, applying the minimalist philosophy to the letter.

Located all alone in a setting as austere as its own design, the building's unassuming, light gray, linear facade hid a wealth of detailing inside that made it perfect for a second home.

Since much of the building's appeal came from its original structure, efforts were made to change it as little as possible.

The ground floor contains a living room, dining room, and kitchen. By the entrance, where before there was a dining terrace, there are now very welcoming twin parlors that make good use of the intense light. In fact, there is a spectacular abundance of natural light which is put to good use throughout the house.

The building's geometric lines contrast with the color and rounded shapes of the surrounding landscape.

Gray is the dominant tone in the living room, with a few dashes of contrasting colors in the decor. Wood and stone prevail in this room, which is centered around the unique fireplace. The room has great dignity, which is enhanced by the two large velvet floor cushions, almost the size of beds, that divide the space. Near them, by the windows, is the dining area, with a sturdy, rectangular table and teak benches. A table from the old restaurant was placed in the simple, functional kitchen.

A sturdy, sukupira wood staircase, hidden behind the chimney, leads up to the second floor, which has a landing, two bedrooms, and a bathroom. Light is a key architectural element here as well. A gap in the staircase ensures that every corner of both floors is brightly lit.

Given the governing spirit of minimalism, the master bedroom, with its dressing room and bath, had to be practical as well as comfortable, with only the essentials. These upstairs rooms have an airy, light-filled, ethereal quality, due partly to the way the rooms flow into each other and partly to the materials used. The predominant neutral gray and white tones are splashed with a few touches of color and decorative accents that humanize the space. The no-nonsense approach is also apparent in the bathroom: the acid-etched, translucent glass in the shower, white walls and ceiling, wooden floor, and metal fixtures are all enhanced by the pure light pouring in.

The designers kept it simple throughout and created a retreat that leaves you yearning to return.

To fully exploit the natural light, the restaurant's old dining room was turned into a double parlor. Although this room is as unassuming as the rest of the project, the mixture of styles is full of warmth and charm.

The gap in the solid, sukupira wood staircase allows light to be distributed equally to both floors.

A room where you are going to rest must be relaxing and cozy. Like the other rooms, the master bedroom has a neutral background, while the textures, decorative touches, and furniture humanize the space and create a sense of well-being.

The entrance leads directly to a large living space overflowing with natural light. The furnishing that fill this plush, relaxing space include an old piano on which a Jaime de Córdoba sculpture sits, a sisal rug, and two velvet floor cushions.

Hidden in a garden

This subtly elegant house is always in touch with its surroundings.

Ibiza, Spain

Modest, restrained, and exotic are perhaps the best ways to describe this house on the Spanish island of Ibiza. The construction plans were clear: stay with the best Balearic building traditions and unpretentious decor, inspired by traditional art and craftsmanship, which would stand up to the passage of time. The designers knew that the building would be bathed in intense light all year round. The result is a charming, open structure, Mediterranean in every sense and, therefore, at one with nature. The boundaries between inside and outside are blurred, its contours allowing refreshing breezes and sunlight to flow throughout the house.

This magnificent residence, so close to nature that plants actually grow over the house in some places, has two floors plus annexes containing the guest bedrooms.

The exterior is painted a light, earthy color to blend in with the plants. On the ground floor, in addition to the main terrace and porch, is a generously proportioned living room. One step up takes you into the dining area, where a corner is occupied by the staircase to the second floor. The harmonious colors are embellished by the plentiful light, which bears witness to the exquisite austerity of the space. The designers knew when to stop: it is decidedly comfortable, but not extravagant.

The ochre tones of the exterior are broken by the white trim around the arched openings in the facade and the lush bougainvillea and hibiscus.

The second floor houses the bedrooms, a bath, and two terraces. The master bedroom has a bed with a wooden headboard and muslin mosquito netting. The obvious ethnic inspiration of this room carries over to the furniture chosen for the adjoining terrace and the country-style bath.

Both the architecture and the decor stem from a pact with nature. In most of the rooms, local traditions are a source of inspiration; the rustic style and simplicity create a comfortable ambience which exudes tranquility.

The main porch, an ideal outdoor dining and living area, is shaded by a climbing plant. The water-filled plastic bags for warding off flies are also conversation pieces.

Detail of the terrace off the master bedroom. The reed roof affords protection from the sun and heat during the long summers. A colonial-style lounge chair and a small stool make a pleasant corner for reading and contemplation.

The many terraces and garden spots permit enjoyment of the outdoors in even the hottest months.

The power of serenity

Shrouded in silence, this peaceful home, with its blend of past and present, invites introspection.

Ibiza, Spain

The architect for this project on the Spanish island of Ibiza, Victor Espósito, that would reflect his understanding of the special setting, had to come up with an impeccable design. And he did: combining yesterday with today so that the house epitomizes the principle that cleverly mixing styles and epochs is a sure way to create uniquely attractive spaces. As a result, the home, while typical of the region, meets every demand of modern society and retains unbeatable charm and austerity.

Well-applied rural minimalism is, in fact, design whittled down to what is beautiful and pure. Here, it is found in a unique Mediterranean context. In this part of the world, light is always a vital element in architecture. It is ubiquitous and must be incorporated into any project. Here, the white walls and the light tones of much of the furniture and many decorative accents intensify the luminosity, which in certain areas is incredibly eloquent.

In the rear of the house, you can look out over a spectacular Ibizan landscape while taking a leisurely dip to cool off.

The rooms are sparsely furnished. Everything inside had to be strictly necessary, practical, simple, and aesthetically pleasing, if not exquisite. These four criteria ensured that the spaciousness of the rooms would be accentuated and that the natural materials employed in the construction would come to the fore.

In addition to a place they would want to call home, the owners also obtained a display case for the rich collection of pieces they accumulated over the years on numerous journeys all over the world. Well aware of the quality and elegance of these beautiful objects, the owners chose to restore most of them and include them as part of the decor. Furniture with a Moorish or classical flair and comfortable contemporary pieces mix in an ambience which shuns luxury and tempts you back every weekend to burn off your stress in the sun, gaze at the horizon, and simply enjoy the unhurried hours: a habit we should all adopt.

Stone, used in most of the buildings on the island, is left exposed on some walls. The natural materials and textures are largely responsible for the rural ambience which prevails throughout the house.

Numerous windows and see-through doors let in a profusion of light which bounces off the lustrous walls, creating an extraordinary backdrop for the furniture and decorative features.

Restored furniture, such as this unassuming colonial rocker, which blends in so well that it is almost camouflaged, is also found in the garden.

Pure style

This house is the product of a relentless search for refinement, for a space where one can appreciate light, balance, and silence

Artà, Majorca, Spain

Simplicity, moderation, and good taste are the hallmarks of this dwelling a few miles outside the ancient town of Artà on the Spanish island of Majorca.

The house, designed by B&B Architecture Studio, was built on the side of a hill, and its two stories take full advantage of the steep slope to offer splendid views, an efficient layout, and luminous, undivided rooms. The objective was to open up the interior space, extend it outward, and, conversely, bring the exterior inside.

This house abandons many conventions. The main entrance is at the back. To the right and left of the door are two independent bedroom suites complete with terrace and bath. After crossing the threshold, you are welcomed to this chaste yet comfortable home by a stunning corridor, in which traditional opaque walls were replaced by glass and wood to exploit the natural light. The colors chosen for the decor are well-suited to the intense brightness, which reaches every corner.

The entry passage has glass walls that take full advantage of the Mediterranean light, which is enhanced by the light tones of the flooring and furnishings.

The entrance hall leads to a spacious, open area containing a combined living room, kitchen, and dining area. A staircase leads up to a second floor, which has another spot for relaxation and the added benefit of a superb panorama of the village of Artà.

The discreet, practical furniture is perfect for ensuring that the space and the house itself are in the spotlight.

The simple, almost ascetic decor provides a
tranquil atmosphere in which it is easy to rest and relax.

The functional, austere furniture, a mixture of country-style and contemporary designs, gives the house its personal feel. Modernity and tradition work together to create alluring contrasts.

The staircase, to one side of the dining area, leads up to a mezzanine-like living room with fantastic views. Painted white and featuring a slender iron railing, its lines are sublime.

Exposed rafters, common on the industrials constructions, are an attractive decorative touch here. The wood, together with the white walls and the iron, is warm and welcoming.

On Majorca, the traditional thick walls and small windows ensure comfortable interiors in both summer and winter.

A renewal of tradition

This sun-drenched Ibizan home renews
exemplary island design while encouraging life in the open air
and enjoyment of nature.

Ibiza, Spain

This house gracefully combines the freshness of the outdoors with the normal comforts expected of any urban home. The original structure was preserved as much as possible; only essential modifications were made, always employing the same type of material that was used when the building was constructed.

The finished product honors the past but has its own special characteristics and all the charm typical of homes on the island. Both the structure and the interior design reflect the Ibizan style, straightforward, warm, and above all natural.

The house, with less than 1,100 square feet of floor space, has thick, whitewashed walls, small windows, stone floors, and wood ceilings, to make it comfortable year-round. The island's rural architectural tradition, which goes back many centuries, focuses on the enjoyment of outdoor living in harmony with nature. The building's lines exemplify the aesthetic simplicity of that tradition and are a response to both the climate and the natural setting. The long hours of sunshine mean that white is used everywhere to offer relief from the heat.

A lovely little corner, where one can take advantage of the shade offered by the many plants growing all around the house, affords shelter from the summer heat.

The furniture is rustic and functional, with only the simplest of ornamental details. Many of the pieces were made on the island and purchased from a local folk art center. Most of the rooms are used for their original purposes, although some were converted to new uses. One of the bedrooms was turned into a convenient dressing room, the corral is now a bathroom, and the granary a guest bedroom.

The house is on two floors, the upper one accessed by a short flight of stairs, and the layout of the rooms is typical for the island. It is intended to be, and is, welcoming, fresh, unassuming, and natural. What is now a

Designed for living, the house preserves the flavor of the past and the fascination of tradition.

small parlor was previously the kitchen. The whitewashed hearth chimney has been preserved and incorporated into the decor.

The house is used mainly on weekends and during the summer, which explains why the kitchen and dining area are outside, sheltered beneath a reed canopy. There is nothing to prevent the residents from enjoying the outdoors.

The simple decor goes hand in hand with the beautiful yet functional rooms. Wood, white walls, and stone, vital to most Mediterranean country homes, are the key ingredients in this cool, unpretentious home.

Thick, whitewashed walls and small windows are a traditional way to beat the heat. The wide window ledges are sometimes used for storage. Above this window is an hiding light.

The interior decoration is restrained and functional. These shelves behind the sofa break the continuity of the white room bathed in natural light.

On one bedroom wall a plank found in the old hayloft serves as a shelf, with similarly reused and restored wooden brackets. A straw basket with a flower arrangement adds a touch of gaiety to the room.

Peerless simplicity

In this house, with no neighbors, surrounded by trees and grass, you can shut out the world and enjoy the stillness.

Majorca, Spain

Empty spaces full of atmosphere, purity, and austerity characterize this home on the island of Majorca. Despite the typically thick walls, light enters through large, modern windows and glass doors. Earth colors and white tones harmoniously combine to create soothing interiors in tune with the setting.

Island craftsmen were commissioned to give shape, in iron, wood, and stone, to architect Thomas Wegner's ideas and sketches. Most of the rooms are on the ground floor, the second story being reserved for a garret-like bedroom. The interior design is completely restrained: a simple bed and a free-standing lamp are the only pieces of furniture.

The flooring in the kitchen and living area consists of rounded stones from the riverbed set in cement. In the rest of the house, polished cement, colored with island soil, was used. The stained pine beam and indigenous reed ceilings are also distinctive. A sturdy iroko wood table with matching benches running alongside occupies the middle of the kitchen. You can look out the windows at the sun-drenched scenery as you work. The counter top is green terrazo, which complements the iron hood and wooden cupboards. The only decorative touches in the room are a wine rack, two candlestick holders (acquired from a local antique dealer), and an oil painting by Majorcan artist Tomeu Pons.

Variety is the hallmark of the kitchen and dining room. The farm-style table and benches, with untreated branches as supports, are illuminated by ultra-modern lamps.

The house sits at the end of a long path, next to a rock that has been spectacularly eroded over the years by torrents of water. One can climb up the steps cut into the rock for a good view of the house's stone exterior, which is characteristic of this part of Majorca.

The clean lines, the refined interior design, and
the richness of the materials used throughout create a relaxing,
monastery-like atmosphere.

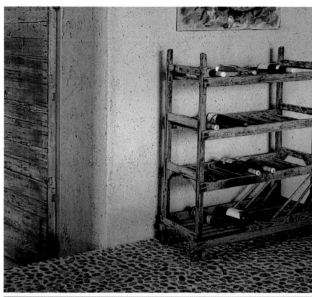

Combining wood (furniture and doors) with the stone floor provides a warm ambience. A few unobtrusive steps separate the different levels of the house.

Some rooms have direct access to the exterior through new iron-framed glass doors. With so much light entering, the boundary between inside and outside disappears.

The ochre walls, earth-colored flooring, and simple furniture create a unique atmosphere. Austerity is pervasive throughout the house.

Locations, Architects and Designers

A farmhouse amid the sunflowers

Williamsport, Pennsylvania, USA

Architect: Aaron Hojman

aaronhojman@hotmail.com

Production: Víctor Carro

Classical inspiration

Santa Rosa, Argentina

Architect: Jacques Bedel

bedel@jacquesbedel.com

Production: Víctor Carro

The perfect hideaway

Avignon, France

Architect: Martín Gómez

gomezarq@adinet.com.uy

Production: Víctor Carro

A magical cabin

Punta del Este, Uruguay

Architect: Juan Ricci

arquamb@ciudad.com.uy

Production: Víctor Carro

A play of contrasts

Firenze, Italy

Production: Dos Ríos

Order and harmony

Punte del Este, Uruguay

Decorator: Patricia Torres

Production: Víctor Carro

Captivating tranquility

Marrakech, Morocco

Architect: Charles Boccara. Estudio de arquitectura en Marrakesch

archiboc@iam.net.ma

The spirit of the millennium

Marrakech, Morocco

Antiquarian: Chez Amidou. Marrakech Medina

The little Alhambra

Palmeral, Marrakech, Morocco

Architect: Charles Boccara. Estudio de arquitectura en Marrakech

archiboc@iam.net.ma

Decoration: Charles Boccara and Natasha Paris

Seduced by the past

Corsica, Italy

Architect: Colombe Stevens

Mediterranean refuge

Lubèron, France

The feel of yesteryear
L'île de Ré, France

An artists' retreat
Saignon in Lúberon, France
Kamila Regent & Pierre Jaccaud
chambreavecvue@vox-pop.net

Minimum expression
Pals, Girona, Spain
Decoration: Augusto LeMonnier
Cristina Rodríguez
Stylist: Ino Coll

Hidden in a garden
Ibiza, Spain
Colonial furniture designer
Lorenzo Queipo de Llano
Stylist: Elena Calderón

The power of serenity
Ibiza, Spain
Architect: Víctor Espósito
Stylist: Ino Coll

Pure style
Artà, Majorca, Spain
Architect: B & B Estudio de arquitectura. Sergi Bastidas
Palma de Mallorca, Spain
bbea@esc-info.com

A renewal of tradition
Ibiza, Spain
Stylist: Elena Calderón

Peerless simplicity
Majorca, Spain
Architect: Thomas Wegner
Weisseshaus, Hamburg, Germany
thomaswegner@gmx.de